MONSTERS

THE MINOTAUR

Other titles in the Monsters series

MONSTERS

THE MINOTAUR

BY MARY SCHULTE

KIDHAVEN PRESS
A part of Gale, Cengage Learning

GALE
CENGAGE Learning™

Detroit • New York • San Francisco • New Haven, Conn • Waterville, Maine • London

GALE
CENGAGE Learning

LIBRARY OF CONGRESS CATALOGING-IN-PUBLICATION DATA

Schulte, Mary, 1958-
    The minotaur / By Mary Schulte.
        p. cm. — (Monsters)
    Includes bibliographical references and index.
    ISBN 978-0-7377-3590-1 (hardcover)
    1. Minotaur (Greek mythology)—Juvenile literature. I. Title.
    BL820.M63S38 2008
    398'.469—dc22

2008006525

KidHaven Press
27500 Drake Rd
Farmington Hills MI 48331

ISBN-13: 978-0-7377-3590-1
ISBN-10: 0-7377-3590-2

Printed in the United States of America
2 3 4 5 6 7 12 11 10 09

CONTENTS

CHAPTER 1

A FIERCE GREEK MONSTER

The ancient Greeks, who lived thousands of years ago, were amazing scientists, philosophers, and warriors. They also were great storytellers. They created stories called **myths** that were filled with gods and goddesses, demigods, monsters, and heroes.

Many of their mythical monsters were **hybrids**, creatures that were part human, part animal. Some of the hybrid creatures included centaurs, sirens, and sphinxes.

Centaurs had the upper body of a man and the lower body of a horse. Sirens had the upper body of a beautiful woman; the bottom part was a bird. The sphinx was part woman, part lion, and part bird.

One of the fiercest hybrid monsters of those ancient days was a creature called Minotauros or Minotaur, who was part man, part bull. Most versions of the myth say the top part of the creature was a bull and the bottom part was a man.

Sharp, pointed horns stuck out from the top of its hairy head. The Minotaur's neck was thick with muscles to hold its large bull head on top of a human body. Some versions of the myth say it had a bull's tail also.

This ancient Greek depiction of a Minotaur was created around 515 B.C.

Unlike ordinary bulls that munched on grass in fields, the Minotaur craved human flesh. It was imprisoned in a **maze** called the **Labyrinth** and fed human **sacrifices**.

Bulls Symbolize Strength

Greek myths often grew from facts or visions. **Artifacts** from early Greece show priests wearing bull masks during religious **rituals**. These rituals may have led to the myth of the Minotaur.

A Minoan fresco depicts ancient toreadors in the sport of bull leaping.

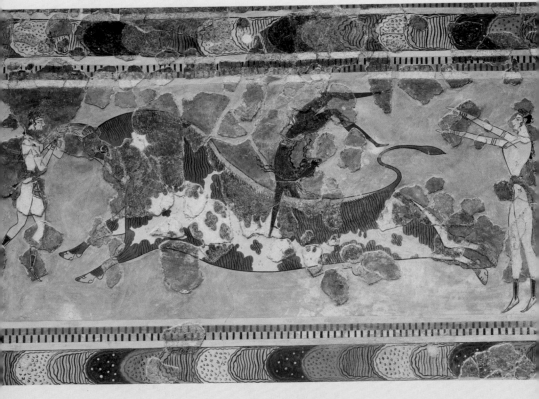

The Minotaur

In many ancient cultures, the bull was a symbol of strength. The Minoans were the earliest European civilization. In the Minoan culture, the bull was a sacred symbol of power. About 4,500 years ago, they built their civilization on the island of Crete. The island is located south of Greece, in the Mediterranean Sea.

The Minoan name comes from Minos, an early ruler of Crete. Their capital city was Knossos. In 1878 the remains of a palace with mazelike floors and many rooms were discovered. Some believe it may have been the setting for the mythical Labyrinth where the Minotaur was imprisoned.

The word *labyrinth* means "house of the double ax."[1] Minoans used double-edged axes in their religious ceremonies. Each ax or "labris" (or labrys or labrus) looked like a butterfly on a stick because of the two sides.

A famous **fresco** from a wall of the great palace at Knossos shows people doing something called "bull leaping." A bull charged headfirst into a line of jumpers. When the bull was right on top of a jumper, the jumper would grab the bull's horns and flip over the bull to land on his or her feet behind the animal. Performing such a **feat** proved great strength.

The bull appears several times in Minoan legends. According to Greek mythology, Zeus, the god of the heavens, saw a young woman named Europa on a beach. He fell instantly in love with her beauty. Zeus magically transformed himself into a magnificent bull. He carried Europa on his back across the sea to Crete.

Europa had three sons with Zeus—Minos, Sarpedon, and Rhadamanthys. Zeus then gave Europa to Asterion, the king of Crete, to marry. Asterion adopted her three sons.

MINOS TRICKS POSEIDON

When King Asterion died, Minos wanted to be king of Crete. He thought he deserved it more than his brothers did. His brothers did not agree—they were ready to fight for the throne. The citizens of Crete were not sure who should be king.

Minos told everyone he could prove that the gods wanted him to rule the kingdom. Then Minos called on Poseidon, god of the sea, for help.

Minos asked Poseidon to send a sign to show his approval of Minos as king. Poseidon sent a strong, white bull to Minos, who promised to sacrifice the bull to honor the sea god. With the god's show of support, Minos became king of Crete.

But King Minos did not sacrifice the gift as he had promised. He switched bulls and sacrificed a different one. The greedy king wanted to keep the magnificent bull for himself.

Poseidon was furious! The gods did not like to be fooled. To punish King Minos, Poseidon cast a spell over Pasiphae, the king's wife. The spell caused Pasiphae to fall in love with the white bull Poseidon gave her husband.

The Minotaur

LXI

A bas-relief sculpture depicts Minos making an offering to Poseidon. Poseidon endorsed Minos's bid to become king, but he became furious after Minos tried to trick the god.

Daedalus Builds a Cow

Pasiphae fell deeply in love with the beautiful white bull. She would do anything to get closer to it. Figuring out how to get nearer to the bull was driving her crazy.

Pasiphae asked the famous architect Daedalus to help her. He was a skilled builder and inventor. He had come to Crete to work for the king. Pasiphae did not tell the king that Daedalus was helping her.

Poseidon was so angry at Minos that he caused Pasiphae, Minos's wife (pictured), to fall in love with a white bull. Pasiphae eventually gave birth to a child that was part bull, part human.

Daedalus built a hollow, wooden structure shaped like a cow. He covered it with the hide of a real cow.

Daedalus put the fake cow into the field where the white bull grazed. He helped Pasiphae climb into the wooden structure so she could be near the beautiful bull.

When Pasiphae eventually had a baby, it was part bull, part human. The Greek scholar Apollodorus wrote: "Pasephae gave birth to Asterios, who was called Minotauros. He had the face of a bull, but the rest of his body was human."[2]

Minotaur means "bull of Minos" (*tauros* means "the bull" in Greek).[3] Minotaur's true name was Asterios or Asterion, which means "starry one."[4]

Sometimes myths have variations. Some versions of the Minotaur myth say the monster had the head and tail of a bull, and the rest of its body was human. Others say the Minotaur had the whole upper body of a bull and the lower body of a human. Still others say its feet were hooves.

On one detail they agree—the mythical Minotaur grew to be a flesh-eating monster.

CHAPTER 2.

THE MINOTAUR AND THE LABYRINTH

King Minos was embarrassed by the Minotaur. He wanted to hide the creature so no one would see it. He did not like it, but he did not kill it because his wife, Pasiphae, loved her bull baby. She wanted to keep it near her and raise it as a child.

The Minotaur could be kept by the queen while it was small, but then it began to get bigger and stronger. It grew sharp horns and hair on its face and upper body. Its grotesque shape scared people, and it began to crave flesh. Finally, King Minos ordered Daedalus to build a cage for the monster.

DAEDALUS CONSTRUCTS A LABYRINTH

Daedalus was a clever builder. He and his son, Icarus, put together a huge underground maze of

14

rooms and winding corridors called the Labyrinth. The Labyrinth had many turns and curves. It was so confusing that no one who entered could find a way out. Only Daedalus knew the secret to get out of the stone prison. King Minos **banished** the Minotaur to the Labyrinth.

Greek hero Theseus battles the Minotaur in the complex Labyrinth built by Daedalus and his son.

The Minotaur was not happy with its new home. It paced and stomped through the twists and turns of the maze. The sounds of it bellowing and roaring could be heard outside the palace. The noise was said to drive people crazy.

KING MINOS DECLARES WAR ON ATHENS

King Minos had a son named Androgeus. The young man went to Greece to compete in the athletic games. While he was there, King Aegeus of

Ships lie in port at Piraeus, which is linked to ancient Athens by a walled road.

Athens sent him on a dangerous mission to kill a wild bull. Instead, the bull killed Androgeus.

King Minos was furious. He declared war on Athens. Destroying the town would be his revenge for the death of his son.

But the Athenians were fierce. They fought back.

King Minos prayed to his father, Zeus, to help him defeat the Athenians. The gods caused drought, **famine**, and sickness in Athens. When the Athenians were weakened, King Minos attacked again. His powerful navy filled the waters around Athens. This time, King Minos took over the city.

Children of Athens Sacrificed

King Minos said he would release the people of Athens from his control if they would pay a tribute. Some versions of the legend say the Athenians had to pay a tribute every year. Other versions say the Athenians paid a tribute every seven or nine years.

The tribute was a human sacrifice. King Minos demanded that seven young men and seven young women be sent to Crete to be fed to the Minotaur. Even though the Athenians did not want to agree to the sacrifices, the gods commanded that they obey King Minos.

A **lottery** was held to choose the victims. Everyone in Athens gathered to see who would be the unlucky seven boys and seven girls chosen for the trip to Crete.

The Minotaur and the Labyrinth   17

The victims would be shut in the Labyrinth, hunted down by the Minotaur, and eaten. If they ran in any direction, they took a chance of running into the Minotaur. If they stood still, the monster might charge out from any corner to grab them. It was impossible to escape.

THESEUS LEARNS OF THE MINOTAUR

A young man named Theseus grew up with his mother and grandfather in the mountains near Athens. No one is sure who the father of Theseus was because Poseidon and Aegeus, king of Athens, were both fond of his mother, Aethra.

Before Theseus was born, King Aegeus left a pair of sandals and a mighty sword under a heavy stone in the mountains. When Theseus grew up and was strong enough to uncover the treasures, his mother told him his father was King Aegeus.

Theseus set off in search of his father. His mother and grandfather begged him to travel by sea, which was the safer route. The road to Athens was dangerous because of monsters and murderers who attacked travelers.

But Theseus was eager for adventure. He wanted to be a hero, like his cousin Hercules. On his journey to Athens, Theseus killed as many bandits as he could.

In this fanciful depiction (opposite), Medea offers Theseus a cup of poisoned wine.

When Theseus reached Athens, he was hailed as a hero for making the roads safe for travelers. No one knew he was really the king's son. Theseus was invited to a fine banquet with King Aegeus and Queen Medea.

The queen knew who Theseus was. She was jealous and feared that he would gain favor with the king. She plotted to have King Aegeus give the young man a poisoned drink.

At the last minute, King Aegeus recognized the sword his son carried. He threw away the poisoned wine and banished Medea, who stormed away in a chariot. King Aegeus introduced Theseus as his son and heir, and the citizens cheered.

But their joy did not last. It was time for the lottery to select the young men and young women to send to Crete to feed to the Minotaur.

VICTIM OR HERO?

Theseus did not want any more Athenian children to die in the Labyrinth. Some say he volunteered to be one of the seven young men sent to Crete. Other versions of the myth say King Minos came to Athens in the ship to watch the lottery. He noticed the handsome young man and chose him to be one of the victims.

Theseus was ready. He told his father he planned to kill the Minotaur. King Aegeus objected, but Theseus was determined. People would look at him as a real hero if he killed the Minotaur monster.

 The Minotaur

Theseus told his father that if he made it out of the Labyrinth alive, he would send a signal. Instead of the black flag of mourning, he would fly a white flag over the ship when it returned to Athens.

Chapter 3

Theseus Battles the Minotaur

Theseus was determined to defeat the Minotaur. He wanted to prove he was a true hero. As Theseus and the other victims set sail for Crete, the black sail of mourning was raised on the ship. The sails unfurled when the wind blew and pushed the ship across the Mediterranean Sea.

Seven young girls and seven young men watched as they neared the shore of Crete. Theseus knew what he had to do, but he did not have a plan—yet.

When the captives arrived on land, they were locked in chains. King Minos told the guards to parade the youths through town while the citizens **jeered**. Theseus stood tall above the other children.

Princess Ariadne Meets Theseus

Among the spectators was Princess Ariadne, daughter of King Minos. When Theseus passed by Princess Ariadne, she fell in love with the brave and handsome young prince. She wanted to rescue him from certain death in the Labyrinth.

Only one person could help Theseus escape the Minotaur. Ariadne called on Daedalus for help, as her mother had done years before.

Ariadne told Daedalus he must show her a way out of the Labyrinth. Then she sent a message to

An early Renaissance painting depicts the story of Theseus. In it, Theseus can be seen fighting bandits (background) and defeating the Minotaur in its maze.

Ariadne, daughter of Minos, gives Theseus a special dagger and a magical spool of thread before he enters the maze to fight the Minotaur.

 The Minotaur

Theseus offering a deal. Ariadne would help him escape the Labyrinth if he would marry her and take her away. Ariadne knew her father would be very angry if she helped the prisoners escape.

Theseus agreed to the deal. He had seen the beautiful princess. Ariadne slipped into the cell where Theseus and the other prisoners were held. She gave him a special dagger and a magical spool of thread to use in the Labyrinth.

THESEUS BATTLES THE MINOTAUR

The next morning Theseus was forced into the Labyrinth with the other captives. He hid his dagger and spool of thread from the guards. At the entrance of the Labyrinth, Theseus tied his spool of thread to the gate so he could find his way back.

The children huddled together in the dark while Theseus hunted for the monster. They did not know who would come around the corner to find them, Theseus or the Minotaur.

The monster knew every inch of the Labyrinth. It knew every corner, every twist and turn. Theseus felt his way along the stone walls. He traveled deeper and deeper into the Labyrinth. As he walked along, he unwound the thread to make a trail back to the entrance.

Theseus could hear the Minotaur panting. A whole year had passed since victims had arrived from Athens. The Minotaur was ready to stalk and kill.

Theseus rounded a corner and came face-to-face with the huge monster. The Minotaur reared his head back and bellowed. Theseus knew he would have only one chance to attack it. Holding his dagger steady, Theseus waited until the Minotaur charged.

When the Minotaur was close enough, Theseus thrust his dagger into the monster's soft neck. The Minotaur roared and crashed to the ground, bleeding. Theseus slashed with his dagger until the Minotaur was dead.

Not everyone agrees that Theseus used a dagger to fight the Minotaur. In another version of the myth, Theseus made his way through the Labyrinth, leaving his trail of thread. He stumbled upon the sleeping Minotaur and killed it with his bare hands.

Theseus followed the thread back toward the entrance. As he stepped around the corner, the children gasped. They cheered when they realized it was Theseus and not the Minotaur. Quickly, Theseus led them out of the Labyrinth.

ARIADNE DEPARTS WITH THESEUS

Ariadne was waiting for Theseus outside the Labyrinth. She and the children left with Theseus on the ship. But first they **sabotaged** the king's ships so they could not follow.

Two versions of the return trip to Athens are told. In one Theseus stopped at an island and took Ariadne ashore. When she fell asleep he left, deserting the young princess who helped him escape.

The Minotaur

Using the dagger that Ariadne gave him, Theseus slays the Minotaur.

Theseus leaves Ariadne sleeping on the isle of Naxos.

The Minotaur

In another version Ariadne was seasick, and Theseus set her on the island of Naxos to recover. When he returned to his ship, a violent wind carried him away to sea. He returned to the island to find her dead.[5]

With so much on his mind, Theseus was not thinking clearly. He forgot to raise the white sail as he had promised his father. King Aegeus sat on the cliff, where he waited each day for news of his son and the other victims.

When the ship sailed closer to Athens, King Aegeus saw the black flag of mourning. He thought his son had died in the Labyrinth. King Aegeus was so sad he threw himself off the cliff and drowned.

To honor the king, the sea was named the Aegean Sea. With the death of his father, Theseus became king of Athens. He was hailed as a hero for bringing the children home safely. The city of Athens prospered under their mighty king.

King Minos, angry that Theseus had escaped, realized that Daedalus was the only person who could have helped him. The king ordered Daedalus and his son Icarus imprisoned in the Labyrinth. Eventually Daedalus crafted wings strong enough for them to fly away and they escaped.

King Minos was not so lucky. His son had been murdered, his prisoners had escaped, his daughter was gone, and his monstrous Minotaur was dead.

CHAPTER 4

THE MINOTAUR IN CULTURE

A hero on a quest, a monster, love, betrayal, and a fight to the death—the myth of the Minotaur and Theseus has all the ingredients of a story that will be told and retold for thousands of years. The flesh-eating monster battling the handsome young Athenian has been drawn, painted, and sculpted through the ages. In books, video games, and movies, the half-bull, half-man Minotaur remains a fascinating creature of strength and **cunning**.

THE MINOTAUR IN GREEK ART

Many vases and household pottery from ancient Greece were decorated with scenes from the popular myths. The Minotaur and his enemy Theseus were used often. A vase from 500 B.C. that sits in the Louvre Museum in Paris, France, shows Queen Pasiphae nursing her son, Minotauros. That unusual image stands out from the many images of the Minotaur in battle against Theseus.

The Minotaur is **immortalized** in bronze and marble in lifelike poses showing Theseus about to

A marble statue by Jeane-Etienne Ramey depicts Theseus slaying the Minotaur. The popular story has been rendered in many different pieces of art.

kill the bull-headed man. A marble statue by Jean-Etienne Ramey in 1826 shows Theseus with a sword above his head, ready to slay the Minotaur, who is on the ground. The marble statue is in the Tuileries Garden in Paris.

The Minotaur is usually shown with the head and tail of a bull and the body of a man. But in the **Middle Ages**, artists often illustrated the Minotaur with a man's head and torso on a bull's body.

Some artists show Theseus killing the Minotaur with a large sword or club, but it seems impossible for him to have smuggled a large weapon into the Labyrinth. Other versions of the myth have Theseus attacking the Minotaur with a dagger or even with his bare hands.

The Minotaur in Picasso's Art

One figure that appears frequently in the art of Spanish artist Pablo Picasso is the bull. Picasso was also fascinated with the Minotaur. The monster shows up in his sketches and paintings from the 1930s. Bullfighting influenced Picasso's work during this period, too. It was a time of great sadness for Picasso. His father died, World War II started, and he went through a divorce.

Pablo Picasso's Blind Minotaur Guided by a Young Girl in the Night *is one of a series of paintings that feature the mythical monster.*

In his series of paintings *Blind Minotaur Led by a Young Girl in the Night* (1934), the Minotaur is a muscular figure with the head and tail of a bull. The world of the Minotaur is dark because of its blindness, but also because it is stuck in the Labyrinth.

In one of the paintings, there is a young girl with a bird in front of the Minotaur, who is resting its hand on her shoulder. In another painting in the series, the girl carries flowers in her arms.

Art historians say that the Minotaur in Picasso's work is often a self-portrait. The Minotaur may be blind in a world of darkness, but it also looks incredibly strong and mighty. Picasso drew thick muscles and a sturdy body for his Minotaur.

MINOTAUR ROCKETS

In January 2000 a six-story rocket shot into space. The official name of the rocket was the Orbital-Suborbital Program Space Launch Vehicle. But its nickname was the Minotaur 1—named after the half-bull, half-man creature because the rocket has two parts joined together.

One part is a retired Minuteman 2 military missile. The other part is a launch rocket. Together, they make the Minotaur 1, a powerful, solid-fuel rocket used to launch small satellites.

The **inaugural** launch of the Minotaur 1 sent a dozen small military and university satellites into orbit. The price tag for the Minotaur 1 rocket was $20 million.

Minotaur 1 launches have put a total of twenty-four satellites into orbit through eleven successful launches. Another eight Minotaur rockets are under contract to perform important U.S. government missions.

The Minotaur

A Minotaur 1 rocket is launched from Vandenberg Air Force Base in California on September 22, 2005.

Minotaur Toys and Games

The Minotaur is a character in the PlayStation 2 game *God of War*. Although the game is not based only on Greek mythology, it does have a world where gods and humans interact. Several of the story lines follow the Greek myths.

Kratos, a Spartan warrior, is the main character. When he reaches the city of Athens, he has to fight creatures that look like Minotaurs. They have the huge head of a bull with a human body. Their weapons are large hammers used for attacking enemies. Many characters in this game have been given greater powers than they had in the myths, but the Minotaur remains true to his mythological character.

In the stuffed toy line for Toy Vault called Here Be Monsters, the Minotaur is a 15-inch-tall (38cm) plush figure. It has beady red eyes and includes a double-sided battle-ax that it can hold in its hand. The ax is shaped like the axes used by the Minoans in ancient Greece.

The Minotaur in Movies and Books

General Otmin is a fierce and bad-tempered Minotaur in the 2005

movie *The Chronicles of Narnia: The Lion, the Witch and the Wardrobe.* Otmin's name does not appear in the book by C.S. Lewis, but there are several Minotaurs in the book.

For the movie, Otmin was created to be the general commander of the White Witch's army. His

A Minotaur named General Otmin is featured in the 2005 film The Chronicles of Narnia: The Lion, the Witch and the Wardrobe.

enemy, Oreius the centaur, commander of Aslan's army, was also created for the movie.

The Minotaurs are heavily armed with two-headed axes and suits of armor. Otmin also has a sword slung on his back. Otmin comes to life through digital effects combined with actor Shane Rangi in a costume.[6]

The second Narnia movie, *The Chronicles of Narnia: Prince Caspian*, was released in theaters in May 2008. Actor Shane Rangi plays a new Minotaur in this second movie. The new character, Asterius, is a good Minotaur who helps Prince Caspian and the Pevensies as they battle King Miraz, who has taken over the throne from his nephew and rightful heir, Prince Caspian.

Like General Otmin, Asterius does not appear in the C.S. Lewis books. He is a character that was added to the story by the filmmakers.

Percy Jackson meets the Minotaur in the *New York Times* best-selling children's novel *The Lightning Thief* by Rick Riordan. Percy and his mother are attacked by a Minotaur on the way to Camp Half-Blood, where Percy learns he is the son of an Olympian god. The teenage demigod defeats the Minotaur by stabbing it with its own horn. But first the monster squashes Percy's mother until she disappears. Percy keeps the horn as a trophy of his battle.

Film rights to the Percy Jackson and the Olympians series have been optioned, and plans are under

 The Minotaur

way for a movie directed by Chris Columbus, who directed the first two Harry Potter films.

With more *Chronicles of Narnia* movies in the works, and the Percy Jackson movies just beginning, the Minotaurs of the future are now in the hands of the creative directors.

NOTES

Chapter 1: A Fierce Greek Monster

1. W.H.D. Rouse, *The Journal of Hellenic Studies*, 1901, p. 268.
2. Apollodorus, *The Library of Greek Mythology*, trans. Robin Hard. New York: Oxford University Press, 1998, p. 98.
3. Pierre Grimal, *The Dictionary of Classical Mythology*. New York: Blackwell, 1986, p. 292.
4. Grimal, *The Dictionary of Classical Mythology*, p. 434.

Chapter 3: Theseus Battles the Minotaur

5. Edith Hamilton, *Mythology*. Boston: Little, Brown, 1942, p. 216.

Chapter 4: The Minotaur in Culture

6. IGN Filmforce, "*Narnia* Exclusive: The Anatomy of a Minotaur." http://movies.ign.com/articles/669/669397p1.html.

GLOSSARY

artifacts: Objects created by humans, usually for a practical purpose, such as a tool, weapon, or ornament of historical interest.

banished: Forced to leave a country or place; driven away; expelled.

cunning: Being wily or tricky; to have ingenuity.

famine: A severe or drastic food shortage.

feat: A notable act or deed, especially an act of courage, skill, endurance, imagination, or strength.

fresco: The art of painting on fresh, moist plaster with pigments dissolved in water.

hybrids: The offspring of genetically dissimilar parents or stock.

immortalized: Exempted from death; not subject to death.

inaugural: The beginning, or the first in a projected series.

jeered: Made fun of, taunted, or teased.

Labyrinth: The place where the Minotaur was imprisoned; a place with intricate passageways and blind alleys; a maze.

lottery: Selection by random drawing; an event whose outcome is or seems to be determined by chance.

maze: A confusing system of tunnels or pathways in which it is easy to get lost.

myths: Stories that people create about heroes, super-human beings, and monsters, in an attempt to explain mysterious events.

Middle Ages: The period of European history from about A.D. 500 to about 1500.

rituals: Religious rites or sacred ceremonies; also tasks that are performed repeatedly, always following the same processes.

sabotaged: Took a deliberate, devious action meant to slow down or stop an opponent or enemy.

sacrifices: Precious things that are given up to gain something more important.

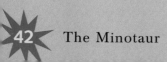

FOR FURTHER EXPLORATION

BOOKS

Ingri d'Aulaire and Edgar Parin d'Aulaire, *D'Aulaire's Book of Greek Myths.* New York: Doubleday, 1962. A comprehensive book of the famous Greek myths, including the Minotaur.

Bernard Evslin, *Monsters of Mythology: The Minotaur.* New York: Chelsea House, 1987. Lively and imaginative telling of the Minotaur story, emphasizing the personalities of the characters.

Alice Low, *Greek Gods and Heroes.* New York: Macmillan, 1985. Many gods and heroes are covered in this book, going back to the beginning.

Scott R. Welvaert, *World Mythology: Theseus and the Minotaur.* Mankato, MN: Capstone, 2005. Easy reader about the famous myth.

WEB SITES

Ancient History: Theseus–Daedalus–Castor and Pollux, About.com (http://ancienthistory.about.com/library/bl/bl_text_bullfinch_20.htm). A respected source for Greek mythology tells the tale of Theseus.

Minotaur Mythweb.com (www.mythweb.com/ teachers/why/fun/minotaur.html). A teacher resource that explains the myth of the Minotaur and Theseus.

***Narnia* Exclusive: The Anatomy of a Minotaur, IGN.com** (http://movies.ign.com/articles/ 669/ 669397p1.html). A detailed look at General Otmin, the Minotaur from the movie *The Chronicles of Narnia: The Lion, the Witch and the Wardrobe.*

Theseus Adventures, Greek Mythology. com (www.greekmythology.com/Myths/The_Myths/ Theseus_Adventures/theseus_adventures.html). The story of the Minotaur, beginning with the adventures of Theseus.

INDEX

PICTURE CREDITS

 About the Author

Mary Schulte is the author of fiction and nonfiction books and magazine articles for children. This is her second book for KidHaven Press. She also is a photo editor and children's book reviewer at the *Kansas City Star* newspaper in Kansas City, Missouri, where she lives with her three children.